Every Kid's Guide to
Understanding
Parents

Written by
JOY BERRY

GROLIER ENTERPRISES INC.
Danbury, Connecticut

About the Author and Publisher

Joy Berry's mission in life is to help families cope with everyday problems and to help children become competent, responsible, happy individuals. To achieve her goal, she has written over two hundred self-help books for children from birth through age twelve. Her work revolutionized children's publishing by providing families with practical, how-to, living skills information that was previously unavailable in children's books.

Joy gathered a dedicated team of experts, including psychologists, educators, child developmentalists, writers, editors, designers, and artists, to form her publishing company and to help produce her work.

The company, Living Skills Press, produces thoroughly researched books and audio-visual materials that successfully combine humor and education to teach subjects ranging from how to clean a bedroom to how to resolve problems and get along with other people.

Managing Editor: Ellen Klarberg
Copy Editor: Kate Dickey
Contributing Editors: Libby Byers, Nancy Cochran, Maureen Dryden, Yona Flemming, Kathleen Mohr, Susan Motycka
Editorial Assistant: Sandy Passarino

Art Director: Laurie Westdahl
Design: Abigail Johnston, Laurie Westdahl
Production: Abigail Johnston
Illustrations designed by: Bartholomew
Inker: Sharon Charlton
Colorer: Sharon Charlton
Composition: Curt Chelin

If you are like most children, you live with a family.

In **EVERY KID'S GUIDE TO UNDERSTANDING PARENTS**, you will learn the following:

- there are different kinds of parents,
- parents want what is best for their children,
- parents are responsible for their children,
- there are many ways parents take care of their children,
- there are several ways parents supervise their children,
- parents deserve to receive something from their children, and
- parents are not perfect.

Your family most likely includes one or two adults who are your parents.

There are many kinds of parents.

Some parents are responsible for the physical birth of their children. These parents are called *biological parents*.

Biological parents are also called "natural parents" or "birth parents."

Not all children live with their biological parents. Sometimes biological parents die or they are unable to take care of their children.

In either situation, the children might be adopted by other adults. When adults adopt children, they promise to take care of the children until the children grow up.

Adults who adopt children are called *adoptive parents*.

Not all children live with biological or adoptive parents. Sometimes one parent dies, and the parent who is still alive marries another person.

Sometimes parents divorce and marry other people. In either situation, a person who marries a parent with children becomes a *stepparent* to the children.

Not all children live with biological or adoptive parents or with stepparents. Sometimes

- both parents die, and it takes time to decide who will take their place;
- parents divorce, and it takes time to decide which parent the children will live with; or
- parents have problems that prevent them from taking proper care of their children.

In any of these situations, children might go to foster homes where they live with *foster parents.*

The foster parents take care of the children until it is decided who will take care of the children permanently.

Most parents *love their children* and *want what is best for them.*

Most parents want their children to be safe.

They also want their children to be healthy and well.

Most parents want their children to learn and become knowledgeable.

They also want their children to be accepted and liked by other people.

Most parents want their children to be happy.

They also want their children to be successful.

In addition to wanting what is best for their children, parents *are responsible for their children.*

If children hurt someone else, their parents are often responsible for seeing that the person who was hurt is taken care of properly.

If children damage something that belongs to another person, the parents are often held responsible for having the damaged item repaired.

If children destroy something that belongs to another person, the parents are often held responsible for replacing the item that has been destroyed.

Because parents want what is best for their children and because they are responsible for their children, parents *take care of their children.*

Most parents do their best to create a good environment in which their children can live.

They also do their best to provide the things their children need.

Most parents do their best to provide good experiences for their children.

They also do their best to help their children survive bad experiences.

Most parents do their best to educate their children. They try to provide their children information that will help them survive and grow.

They also try to teach their children what is acceptable and unacceptable behavior.

In addition to taking care of their children, parents *supervise their children.*

Most parents do their best to encourage their children to behave responsibly.

They also establish guidelines that tell their children how to act and what to do. The guidelines are called *rules*.

Most parents enforce the rules that have been made. This means that they make sure the rules are respected and obeyed.

One way parents enforce rules is by *talking* to their children.

Another way parents enforce rules is by *letting their children suffer the consequences* of breaking the rules. This means the children have to experience whatever happens to them as a result of breaking the rule.

Another way parents enforce rules is by *punishing* their children.

One kind of punishment is *isolation.* This means putting the child somewhere where he or she is alone.

A second kind of punishment is *deprivation.* This means taking something away from the child that he or she really likes.

Taking care of children and supervising them require a great deal of time and effort. Parents deserve to receive something in return from their children.

Here are some ways you can repay your parents for the things they do for you.

1. Put yourself in your parents' place.

Try to understand why they think and feel the way they do. Then try to respect their thoughts and feelings.

2. Accept your parents the way they are.

Do not try to get them to change.

3. Show your appreciation for your parents.

Tell them how much you love them and praise them whenever you can.

4. Encourage your parents when they are discouraged.

Tell them they are doing OK. Say things that will give them hope and confidence to keep trying.

5. Help your parents establish and enforce the rules.

Help your parents set up the rules. Then cooperate with these rules.

6. Talk to your parents calmly and honestly when you disagree with them or are upset about something.

Avoid nagging or arguing with them.

7. Admit when you do something wrong or make a mistake that affects your parents.

Tell them you are sorry. Ask them to forgive you.
Try not to make the same mistake again.

8. Try to make your parents feel OK when they do something wrong or make a mistake.

Try to forgive them. Then do your best to forget their wrongdoing or mistake.

9. Help your parents any way you can.

Ask your parents, "What can I do for you? Is there anything I can do to help you?"

10. Do something special to show your parents you love them.

A good rule to follow is to treat your parents the way you would want to be treated if you were them.

Most parents do what they do for the right reasons and in the right way.

However, parents are people and are not perfect. Sometimes parents can be unfair or unkind.

Talk to your parents calmly if they are ever unfair or unkind. If this does not help the situation, cooperate with your parents as best you can.

If you are fair and kind with your parents, chances are they will be fair and kind to you most of the time.

No matter what kind of parents you have, they most likely do a great deal for you and deserve to have you treat them with kindness and respect.